This book is
dedicated to the memory of

_____

wish you were here!

For Chloe Liv
Based on a true story

Words and pictures by Andy Cohen
Edited by Tiffany Markman

Contact Andy Cohen: andy@globalmicro.co.za; facebook.com/StoriesThatMatter2U | Layout by Creative Heroes | All rights reserved. No part of this publication may be reproduced in any form or by any means (electronic, photocopying, recording or otherwise) without prior written permission of the author. Any person infringing these rights will be liable to prosecution and civil claims.

A lady with a round belly
Tended to her blooms,
Thinking all about how she
Would be a mom quite soon.

And as she pottered
In the shade of a tree
A bee buzzed about
Keeping her company.

And while she felt so truly blessed,
For all the things she had,
The lady couldn't help but think
How much she missed her dad.

She remembered their talks
And how he'd say
How much he'd love
**Grand-kids one day.**

And with a baby en route;
With one well on the way,
It just felt wrong that
He couldn't come play.

They sat together in her dream,
A **daughter** with her **dad**,
And she said she couldn't help
Just feeling really **sad**.

I'm thinking and thinking
Of a whole list of things…
Doing them **without you?**
That really kind of **stings!**

It's not right that you
Won't meet this tot.
Because you won't get to spoil her
With the gifts you've got.

To which Dad replied,
But spoil her I can!
Just not with the things
In my original plan...

Oh, the things that
She'll **receive** from **me**!
The best of the best,
Just wait and see...

But instead of teddies,
More than dolls and sweets galore,
More than a wendy house
With toys across the floor...

Instead of boxes filled
With building blocks
Or wardrobes stuffed with
Fancy frocks...

I've got more precious gifts to bear.
Presents of real value to share:

Knowledge, courage and an imagination.

An exceptional life, with no limitation.

Warmth and strength and talents, too.

A long, full life with her dad and you.

These are the presents
That have the most worth,
Which I could not send her
If I were on earth.

So when you look at your child
And in her you see
All her bountiful blessings…

Well - they are from **me!**

As the bee and its buzz
began fading away...
The lady then realised
Why Dad could not stay.

She opened her eyes.
What a dream she'd just had!
She touched her hand to her belly
And felt a little less sad.

# Talking to Kids about Loss
## A note from the author

We never get over losing someone. The nature of grief is that we revisit that loss at different times in our lives, in new roles and from fresh perspectives.

In my case, I lost my father when I was 21 and mourned him as a child who had lost her father. Then, 11 years later I felt it all over again, but differently. This time I grieved as a mother, whose daughter would never get to meet her grandfather. And so I decided to comfort both of us by helping my child get to know her grandfather through my memories.

This has helped me process my grief and introduced my daughter to her late Grampa, and somewhere in all of that, she will be eased into understanding how life works.

My wish for this book is that it helps families, caregivers, teachers and mental health practitioners to address loss with children in constructive, proactive and loving ways.

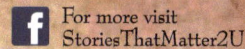

For more visit
StoriesThatMatter2U

## Some helpful processes:

**1. Read this book** and talk about what it feels like to miss someone. Make a list of the things you remember about the person. Draw a picture together of what you would like that person to know. Don't be afraid to be sad together!

**2. Plant seedlings** in the garden. Give the plant a name and encourage your child to visit, tend and even talk to it, often. The garden has a wonderful way of gently teaching us about beginnings and endings.

**3. Make a snow globe picture-frame:**

### Materials:
1 x clean glass/plastic jam jar
1 x photo of that special someone
1 x glitter pot
Silicone-based glue
Water
Some coloured markers, ribbons, bits and bobs

**Directions:** Gently curve the photo around the inside of the jar so that the image faces the centre of the container. Stick the back of the photo in place with a few drops of silicone-based glue. Fill the jar with water and sprinkle in a teaspoon of glitter. Wipe away any excess water, screw on the lid and seal it with silicone. Decorate the outside of the jar together - sharpies work really well but you can use any bits and bobs to embellish the jar. Now encourage your child to shake, interact and play with this whimsical and personal artwork. This is a really useful tool for parents to contain open-ended questions and to generate a sense of calm around 'not knowing' all the answers.

## About the Author

Andy Cohen is an arty lady who loves to create stories about things that really matter. She is trained as a Psychoanalytic Community Art Counsellor, which is just a fancy way of saying that she creates safe spaces for non-arty people to talk, create and feel heard.

Andy is also an artist and has extended her Fine Art skills to Masters level. She currently lives in South Africa surrounded by her sassy family, her rambunctious dogs and lots and lots of art supplies.